Daycare Days for Providers

What You Should Know Before Opening

Your Home

Miko Marsh

Table of Contents

Introduction

Welcome! Come on in and get settled. We have several things to cover, and you're going to want to be comfortable as we discuss these topics. This book is designed to fill in some gaps and answer questions before they become highly uncomfortable situations that force you to come up with an answer on the spot. I discovered that I could either learn quickly from the experience of others, or I could take extra time and learn through my own costly mistakes. I did both. I applied what other providers had learned, and I learned the hard way when I met new situations. There are several good books already out that will tell you how to start a home daycare or center, and there are a couple books and articles giving you information about basic operations and day-to-day schedules. This book helps bridge some of the technical information of "how to open" a business to "what to expect" day-to-day as a daycare provider. It answers questions not often answered and gives mentoring advice to the newbie and to the one that has had some experience already.

I'm the kind of person that enjoys giving back to the community and helping those coming up behind me. I have this in place so we can discuss situations to which new providers often don't give thought until they've already gotten themselves stuck. I want to help you avoid the quicksand and guide you to a steady path.

You may be thinking, "Why didn't you just give me the book for free if you want to help me so much?" Well, I have a few reasons.

1. We tend to pay more attention to things when we've invested something of our own into it. When you purchase the book, you're more likely to take heed and make mental notes. If you're focused the first time, you won't have to backtrack later.

2. Tips, ideas, support, etc. can be found as we add them online. The book has more in-depth information on some topics because I am focused on helping fellow providers improve their business. Writing the books take more time and effort, so cost it me a lot behind the scenes to get it to you.

3. You can use this as a tax write-off for your business, so you will receive some benefit from buying it.

Let me tell you a little about myself. I have provided child care or assisted in providing child care for someone every year of my life since I was knee-high to a grasshopper. I baby-sat for years. I worked or volunteered as an assistant in a corporate nursery, non-profit daycare center, two large family daycares (including 24-hour care), and worked as a nanny. I have operated as an unlicensed, registered, and military licensed provider. I waited six years before opening my own daycare because I wanted to research, study, and make sure I was prepared to enter this career. I first opened my doors as licensed provider in July 2005. I also work in the mental health field when I choose to work outside the home. I have a degree in psychology with a minor in counseling. Typically, I work with youth that exhibit several behavioral, social, emotional, and/or sexual disorders as a residential counselor. I have also worked with suicidal/homicidal patients in a hospital setting. This does not include the different jobs and volunteer experiences I had along the way.

My average work week is about 75 hours if I have a standard 50-hour child care week. When I've needed to be outside the home, I've used baby-sitters and daycare facilities. I am speaking as someone who has operated as a daycare provider for several years and as a parent who has needed daycare. I am hoping you get something informative from this book to further you in your career and that you will gain some understanding as to how a parent might react to some situations you may have. I let people know upfront that I am Christian. My operations reflect my faith since I am as much a Christian as I am a woman. Since I'm sharing what I've learned, I'm also sharing things I applied spiritually as well (under "passage to ponder"). You're welcome to read or skip those sections. There's no test at the end of this book, so you're not under pressure to answer questions. They are for the benefit of those that appreciate it.

That's my introduction. Now let's talk business.

Section 1: In the Beginning

Baby-sitting ≠ Daycare

I got it. You helped out with your little brother a couple times while you were growing up. You watched some neighborhood children once a month. Your aunt got you special permission to help in the center where she works once a week last year. You monitor the church nursery for two hours every week. Wonderful. However, that's not enough to adequately prepare you to operate your *own* daycare because it's not a true picture of what it's like to do this on a daily basis. The apartment complex you used to live in could have voted you the best baby-sitter of 2010, but it really means very little on this end.

When you baby-sit, you generally go to *other people's* houses, prepare *their* food, watch children in *their* home, use *their* electricity & water, utilize *their* toys & furniture, get paid an hourly wage, and go home. You might baby-sit in your home, but not much is

5

different. Times are usually for short periods. Baby-sitters tend to charge about $10/hr. Most daycare providers don't earn minimum wage. Many of us provide all the meals, snacks, and drinks for children, pay our utilities, buy our own toys & supplies, replace things that get damaged, and look at daycare 24/7.

<u>Daycare is not for you if</u>:

- ➢ You are looking for a fast buck.

    - Plan on not breaking even for a long time. You can't open & close shop when you don't see the earnings you need. Realistically, you will be starting in the hole. You can utilize free resources such as the library or a loan library, but you will need to come out of your pocket. If you must get a loan, you may need to draft a business plan first. You will need to check with your city/county to understand zoning laws and regulations for operating a home business.
    - You may need specific certifications before you are even considered as a provider. Many states have outlined minimum requirements to operate legally as a provider. The days of just sitting in your house and watching the neighborhood kids are over. Child care providers often have the same qualifications as licensed preschool teachers, so you will be expected to do more than just sit them in front of a television and keep them alive until their parents return.
    - If you want to earn any income – much less a living – then

you will need to market, promote, and sell your services. Everything you need to run a daycare has to be in place before your doors open.

➢ You can't manage time, discipline yourself, or learn how to get organized.

- Families depend on you to be available when you say you will be. If you come across as "all over the place," people will not trust you. Get it together! You will have very long days, which typically run 10-12 hours daily just for child care. This does not include washing dishes, sanitizing toys, cleaning the home, planning menus, buying groceries, shopping for toys, organizing activities, preparing paperwork, reviewing charts, conducting interviews, etc. Plus, you have to do things for your family, too. If you plan to "wing it," you will find yourself freefalling without a parachute.

➢ You don't like children or working with people.

- This is complete social interaction. If the idea of children touching you or people talking to you gets on your nerves, you might be better off in the back office somewhere. Seriously, I don't know how many people I've met that swear up and down that they'd make good daycare providers, yet they don't have a clue how to interact with children and have unrealistic expectations of parents. Just because you like *your* children doesn't mean you like *other people's* children.

➢ You have no sense of commitment.

- Children need stability, and you may be the only stable person they have. You can cause attachment problems by taking on children and closing because you feel like trying another career. One of the most frustrating things I come across as a provider is reading or listening to moms that decide they want to watch kids for a while to earn extra income. In all honesty, that's fine, but don't promote yourself as a daycare provider because you aren't. If I got an average hourly pay for all the hours I volunteered, assisted, worked, studied, and trained (not including time caring for my own children), I could send all of my children to the colleges of their choice, give them new cars as gifts, and purchase a new house.

- I'm not saying moms shouldn't watch children (unless they're endangering children). The problem I see is that they usually don't stick it out for more than a few months, if that long. Deployed husband returns, and mom closes shop because she just needed a few dollars and something to keep her occupied until her husband returned. If you let people know upfront that this is temporary, then there should be no problems. However, telling families they have two days to find permanent care is highly inconsiderate.

➢ You aren't willing to abide by laws.

- One of the reasons we have so many restrictions now is because people don't use common sense. You are responsible for the lives of other people. That is not a responsibility to be taken lightly. If you want to "do your own thing," go do something else. Even if you don't think about the fact that many homes are not child-proofed, there should be no reason for some of the headline horror stories we have to read. My child should not be sitting or playing inside any large appliance. Children have suffocated because they could not get out. Be sober. I'm not paying you to pass out and allow my child to wander out of the house and down the street. You're licensed for six children because you don't have enough space for 23. You're almost four times over your limit. Please take this position seriously. People have fought for years to get you support and recognized as a hard-working professional.

➢ You are not ready to operate as a business.

- Clients are not going to just fall from the sky. You have to study, plan, plot a course of action, determine your financial spending, set up, determine policies, advertise, interview, and maintain clients. You are solely responsible for if you get paid *at all*!

- Working as an employee and being self-employed are two entirely different ballgames. As an employee, you get paid for a set amount of hours you work, you report to someone else, and there is someone above you in the chain-of-command if there is a problem. When you are self-employed, the buck stops with YOU. You may spend 100+ hours a week on your business and still not earn two nickels to rub together. You have to examine the good (everyone sees money) and the bad (profit loss). You need to figure out how you're going to stay afloat while you try to turn a profit.

- You cannot let your heart override your business sense. If you're here "just for kicks" but don't think you could stand up to a parent or enforce your policies, you'd be better off volunteering somewhere.

➢ You want something simple that doesn't require work.

- If you want peaches 'n cream, go order a dessert. Business ownership isn't for everyone, as many former workers will tell you. Many small businesses fold in the first year. If you're afraid of rejection, can't handle failures or setbacks, or don't think you are ready to handle responsibility and give it your all, then don't set yourself up for a huge disappointment.

If you want the freedom to come and go as you please, to decide if and when you will work, and don't want to be held to many expectations, then continue baby-sitting. If you are ready to branch out as an established business owner, then roll up your sleeves, and prepare to get your hands dirty. We're here to support you, but I'm not going to sugarcoat the foundation. You need to know what to expect so you can prepare to handle it. You can do it, but you need to settle it within yourself that you're going to put forth a true, steady effort.

Passage to ponder – Luke 14:28-33 Count the cost.

The same way Christ told His followers to understand what discipleship meant is the same way we can look at this for other areas of our lives. Consider everything that you need to supply to build and maintain your business.

Are you thinking about it? Have you decided to move forward? Let's go!

Know Your Limits

Providers sometimes tend to forget that we're not superwomen. Although we have to wear many hats – teacher, caregiver, dietician, and so forth – we don't run on batteries or come with the ability to download expertise in a field on the spot.

It's easy to burn out when you don't take time for yourself or make down time. Make sure you use your days off to recuperate. When you continue to pick up additional hours, the pay doesn't seem to match your exhaustion. Days become endless, and sometimes, people don't understand.

I have offered odd hour care. During one of my certifications, I worked an average of 60 hours week and carried 15 credit hours, which meant I had about another 50 hours of study time. My work week would be 10-hour days Mon – Fri and two overnights/extended-hour care. The next season, I had multiple 90+ hour work weeks back-to-back trying to be available and earn an extra dollar. At one evening pickup, the mother mentioned bringing her daughter on a federal holiday, which was a couple days away. I reminded her that I'm closed on federal holidays. After I tried to explain, she got angry and left. I ended up offering to help for school that day but explained I couldn't be available that weekend since I would have worked almost 4 weeks straight at 90+ hours each week with *no* break. She had the choice of child care for school or weekend care for her job, but I was running on the last bit of energy I had left and couldn't go without a day of rest.

People tend to assume that providers sit around all day watching TV, eating, and sleeping. They forget that we're running a business. Just because we're home doesn't mean we get to do whatever we want. If I want to hop in my car and shop for groceries, I can't without parental consent. I can't relax in my home the way I can when I don't have to spend hours on end on alert to avoid dangers or things that might upset the parent of someone else's child. Even when I'm hosting a sleepover, I'm in the same room with the children in case someone gets sick or scared during the night. I usually fall asleep almost 3 hours after they do and cat nap throughout the night because I'm listening for the slightest disturbance. That's not rest or all fun and games. It's mentally and physically taxing.

- Take breaks. Schedule rest. Get adequate sleep. Learn how to say "no." If you don't, your body will do it for you, and you will shut down when you least expect it.

I had a client who was severely autistic. I had worked with a couple of children with autism before but really had no idea of the challenges they and the family faced until this child was enrolled. I very quickly discovered that I was in over my head and could not

13

meet this child's needs because I did not have the training to help me face each episode. I truly wanted to make it work because I did not want to turn anyone away and wanted to be available for the family; however, I realized that since I was so inexperienced, I would only be experimenting with her while trying to help. I was afraid I would do more damage than good by keeping her, so I offered the family assistance in finding another provider and professional support. I was tearful and absolutely heartbroken behind the whole situation, but I had to recognize my limits and consider the needs of the child.

Had I met with both the parent and child ahead of time (I had enrolled the child without meeting with her first), I could have spared everyone stress. I would have been able to inform the mother that I mainly deal with children who are actively trying to harm others. My specialty is not in cognitive functions, so the best thing I could do for her was to give her a list of providers who had training and extensive experience working with autistic children and agencies that either had extensive knowledge and resources for families or those which could put her directly in touch with them.

- If you do not have the knowledge, capability, or facility required that can meet a child's needs, then you owe it to that child to point the family to someone who can. DO NOT take the risk of causing a major setback because you want to "try it out." If there are providers who can better care for the child, do not keep the child because you want her tuition.

Passage to ponder Matt 18:10

We are to care for the spiritually young as well as those who are physically young. We are responsible for our leadership and will be held accountable for steering them wrong or bringing them harm.

What Is Your Target Age Group?

What ages do you enjoy the most? You may like something about each age, but it is difficult to start off across the board with ages 0 – 12. In fact, I would advise against it.

1) You need to take into account your usable daycare space. Infants require more space.

2) You need to be able to plan activities for them.

If you aim for infants to preteens, you will have to have enough supplies for each age group. For the younger ages, you'll need multiples to avoid fighting over toys. Something new providers tend to focus on is how many children they'd ideally like to be able to enroll to earn a profit. That can cause you to overshoot your current situation. Don't focus on the ideal but rather what is needed to support you.

Let me try to help. Look around your home, and imagine children in the space you have for daycare. Can you see it? I'm willing to bet they're all sitting quietly and behaving themselves in your mind. Now, let's say you want eight children. You can only have two infants in your mixed-age group. Let's say you have a 6-month-old rolling over, a 17-month-old that has discovered the joy of running and climbing on furniture, twin 4-year-olds, and four after-school kids who are with you. When the 9 and 10-year-olds stand up, do you still feel like you have enough space? What about when the toddler bolts? If you are new to this end and do not have an assistant, find a provider in your area that has about as many children as your desire, and ask if you can sit with her to get guidance as to how to manage care.

If you prefer babies, you might want to set up your home tailored as an infant home. If you prefer preschoolers, then you'd arrange differently. If you focus on older kids, you'll need things that would interest them such as board games or science projects instead of Mr. Potato Head and 4-piece puzzles. Knowing which ages you plan to keep will make shopping much easier.

Section 2: Setting up Your Daycare

<u>Getting Started</u>

There's no reason not to think big! The thing to remember is that you have to take things one step at a time. If you're in an area that will allow you to operate where you are, that is a great place to start. You do not have to have a 2500 sq ft house with the entire bottom floor dedicated to daycare, murals throughout, built-in personal shelves, and a $6000 mini amusement park in the back yard. While that sounds like a great setup, that's not what I mean when I say you need everything in place before you get started. You don't want to overextend yourself. Even if you're looking for a home with daycare in mind, think about things for the long-term, but do not try to attack everything at once.

When I opened one of my locations, I was also looking for a home that would make a good investment based on the build, location, and improvements being done in the area. I took out a loan to cover the first few months of rent, buy furniture, purchase toys, and pay for licenses, taxes, and trainings. I liked the house, but I rushed in without bothering to get advice about what I should check and would need to operate there. I had already learned I could get zoned for care and made sure my lease stated I had permission to operate a daycare. Shortly after I moved in, I learned the wiring was poor. An electrician had to come out because the fuse would short and only allow 25% of the house to be lit. He guessed the exact age of the house based on the wiring, which he said would have burned the house down eventually trying to hold the charge. Weather temperatures were over 95 degrees, so not having air conditioning was extremely difficult. (If you have a child with asthma, you are required to have air conditioning.)

My next discovery was that I could not get my city permit because the house hadn't passed inspection to be a rental property. The inside and outside of the walls had to be painted, the radiator needed to be fixed, and a few other things had to be done before the city would okay it. My phone number was working the first day, but I couldn't find the phone jacks downstairs. I got a cordless with an extra phone to work around the issue until a repairman could check the line. I discovered the phone lines downstairs were corroded, and I couldn't have a phone line downstairs unless I paid for a second line. (Mind you, I'd been in the house less than 2 weeks total when I learned about all of this.) I found a dryer at a garage sale and bought a brand new washing machine. However, the technician informed me that while there were washer/dryer hookups in the add-on room, there was no pipe connection to catch the water on the spin cycles. This meant that every time I washed clothes, I had to be at the washing machine each time the spin cycle came on so that I could pull the hose from the wall and hold it over a bucket and then dump the bucket. I discovered a large toy bin would hold the water from two regular size spin cycles or one super load spin cycle. I used a bucket to scoop from the bin to the toilet every time I washed clothes for the entire year I was there. My arms and back became very toned.

New daycare provider orientation was offered once per month, and I had to get everything in place so I could apply for licensing within 30 days after the session. Although I was still employed full-time (don't quit your day/night job yet!!), I was now more than two months behind my schedule for opening. I had a rotating shift, so I couldn't take just one child and quit. However, I had switched to PRN status, which meant I could give my availability and work if there was an opening. Thankfully, there was always a shift available for me. When it was time for my inspection, I was assigned one of the rudest monitors I'd ever met. Long story short, she told me immediately that I wouldn't pass inspection based on the fence and that she'd go through everything else. She'd only been there four minutes, so I didn't understand why she'd put me through another 236 minutes of frowning and complaints.

Obviously, I didn't get my license that day. I had several more things to address that I wasn't aware were concerns.

The following month, I was state certified but no longer had a running vehicle to get to work. I was way behind getting income and had already paid back over $1000 on my loan. Having state approval permitted me to be listed with the Child Care Resource & Referral, which helped with getting noticed. I needed the edge because I had totally missed the fact that I chose to move onto the exact same block as a home that had been certified as a center. I was literally 6 houses down from her!! On the other side of me was the elementary school. I discovered they offered an after-school program, which made it that much harder to persuade parents to use my program. The only way I could compete would be to offer at least the same rate, which was $12.50/week/child! Sitting smack dab between a center for preschoolers and an afterschool program that takes a few dozen children created an immediate challenge with getting clients, so I promoted my infant availability and evening hours. God was kind enough to send me a couple families almost immediately.

So, I was finally operating my daycare full time, but I had repairs that needed attention, and the heater went out downstairs. During many days, I had to get up at 5am to prepare to warm up the house. It would be 75 degrees upstairs and would be 20 degrees colder by the time I hit the bottom of the stairs. I turned on all the lights, made sure the curtains were pulled to cut down on draft from the window, turned on a portable heater, and used the oven to help warm the middle of the house. My electricity bills averaged a little over $400/month during winter. My utility bills were one of the reasons I worked 80 - 100 hours/week. In addition to all the surprises that kept coming up, I had installed an alarm system with a company that gone out of business (I wasn't notified). I had also signed up to take credit card payments because I thought it would make things simpler. It didn't and ended up costing me more than I had expected due to monthly fees.

So…learn from my very expensive experience. Plan and budget with a small cushion of savings just in case you run into setbacks, additional problems, or get no clients for a while. My primary mistake was that I believed I wouldn't be recognized as a "real" daycare and couldn't get certified if I wasn't in a house. I let my assumptions burn a hole in my pocket, and I tried to take on too many projects at once. While it would be fantastic if things just fell into place perfectly on schedule, it often doesn't happen that way. Inspections may be delayed, weather conditions may not be suitable for outdoor repairs, licensing may take longer to approve you, background checks may take several weeks, required classes may not be available until the next season, the time you open may not be ideal for gathering clients because they're already enrolled in programs, etc. Hope for the best, but have backup plans in place.

Daycare Space: Yes, Your Apartment or Townhome Could Work

I have used entire downstairs spaces for daycare and have used one primary room for daycare. I have not suffered for lack of clients with any setup. Part of the fun of daycare is arranging furniture, especially if you like the new looks that are created.

Look #1 (2 other rooms are used also)

Look #2 (combined 2 rooms of furniture & moved my desk & computer – not seen above)

Here are a couple of ways to maximize space when you have a smaller area:

The top row is one arrangement over two rooms (I had at least a dozen different arrangements). Notice, I used part of the hallway to store books. Since the fireplace was not being used, I blocked it off to conserve heat, prevent little ones from playing with it, and to make the most of my area. This arrangement gave me the most space for infants to crawl safely. The bottom row shows the same two rooms used when the youngest were walking/running, and I had preschoolers enrolled.

(Take note: Use a real camera to promote your daycare pictures unless a camera phone with poor picture quality is all you have available.) This area was rearranged several times also. Even if you have big furniture, you can work around it. The piano is aligned against the wall of the hallway because it was a wide walkway. You can see part of the piano in the top left corner of the upper middle picture. I used shelves to divide the room and used the couch to help create a quiet place for reading.

As you can see, the space isn't the primary factor – it's what you bring to what you already have that makes the difference!

Miko Marsh

Passage to ponder – Matt 25:14-30

What has the Lord given/made available to you? Are you going to work with what you have or just wait for something to happen? Don't expect the big things to come to you before you've shown you can handle the little things. Use what you have, and make it work to the best of your ability.

Section 3: Interpersonal Relationships

Avoid Letting Relatives Be Clients

Obviously, this is not a hard and fast rule – just advice. Relative care is wonderful, especially when children are infants. You know that your family is in good hands with someone who genuinely loves that child. The reason we usually advise against it is because it is difficult to have a business relationship with family. The two don't even out.

- Many times, providers are expected to give a discount to relatives even though they are expected to receive the same activities, guidance, food, and privileges as the other clients. While you may be able to provide this service at a discounted rate as a courtesy, you may not be able to maintain holding that spot when you could receive a regular rate for another client. A discount usually means money out of your pocket.

- Some relatives feel that they can speak to you as if they don't have any sense. While many parents tend to view child care providers as their personal employees, relatives tend to take extra liberties because they feel they have a level of familiarity that gives them the right to be disrespectful to you because you "have" to love them.

- You will feel obligated to turn down potential long-term clients to make accommodations for your grandchild, niece, nephew, or cousin. Relatives do not want to sign contracts because they do not want to make a commitment to your daycare. You are there until they can find something they like better. This means that your income is always uncertain because you don't know when they will just stop paying you. This is hardest when you have turned down new clients or asked current clients to find alternate care because their schedule conflicted with the family schedule. You lose twice, and the relative walks away totally unaffected and carefree.

- There is a great chance that you will get late and partial payments regularly when you need them the most. Family takes liberties to use money that is for you to go to things they need to pay or want to buy and expect you to be okay with their allocation of funds because they believe you can wait, especially when they believe you can afford to not get paid because you operate a business.

- Guilt trips are often run on family members. They will say that you not providing additional services and care on-demand tells them that you don't care about how hard they have it. You suddenly become unloving and mean when you don't provide that extra day of care of which you had already planned to be closed. The long hours you put in, your being tired, and having your own worries are nowhere near close to the difficulties they are facing. You not giving them what they want means that you have joined the whole wide world in taking sides against them.

- You will feel increasingly irritated if you discover that while you believed you were watching a child an additional 24 hours on top of your regular wcck so your relative could go to work, he or she was actually partying in a club somewhere. If you want to watch the child so he or she can do that, it's fine. But if you find out you were guilted into providing care so that person could hang out, you're going to find yourself avoiding him or her because you were used.

- Your relationship will be strained. There will be times of tension because your desire to go into daycare mode will make it difficult to wait for the parent to take action to correct or ensure the safety of the child. The parent might expect you to take action to correct or ensure the safety of the child whenever the child is near you, which deprives you of a break when you're just spending time together.

There are times it can work out long-term, but you need to have ground rules laid out so you don't get the short end of the stick. You will be expected to be flexible on your rules, so you have to protect yourself so you don't break down physically, mentally, financially, or splinter your relationship.

Nobody Cares about Your Business as Much as You Do

It's not that "nobody cares" about your daycare, but nobody has as much vested interest in this as you do. Let's examine a few things.

Parents look out for themselves:

Can you blame them? Their first priorities are to do what works for them and their families. Parents tend to choose providers based on rates, hours, location, benefits to them, and ratio of children to provider. Other things, such as the provider's personality are major factors, but the first questions they ask revolve around the question "What can you offer *me*?" Sometimes you will have the wonderful experience of finding parents that "care" about you and genuinely interact with you; however, their loyalty lies with their family and not with you, which means that if they need to change providers because you or they moved too far away, don't count on them for another year of tuition. They may prefer you, but they will get over having to get a new provider quickly.

With that said, you also need to consider the flip side of that good relationship. You will encounter parents that believe their preferences override your policies. They may send children to care eating chocolate or fast food and expect you to let Little Tommy eat at the table while you're doing crafts. Your rule states "no outside food," but Mom didn't want to hear her son cry and expects you to let him have his chocolate (exposing your daycare child with allergies to health issues) or to be the bad guy and take it from him. You may have someone leave with no notice, which leaves you unable to fill that spot for a while because you did not have time to advertise creating a loss in income.

<u>Your assistant will go to sleep first</u>:

Can you blame her? The business has *your* name on it, parents go to *you* for serious issues, and *you* will take the biggest hit if you have no business. Your assistant may feel some of the hit, especially if she lives in the house and the income pays the mortgage, BUT…she can go find another job. You have to decide what you're going to do to get your business going again.

She doesn't have the training you have. You were the one that attended hours of orientation, spent your tax return on college classes, bartered child care for car repairs, worked odd hours around the clock at multiple jobs, and used "free time" to buy toddler toys in order to get your business off the ground. You can't expect her to remember what's in *your* head. You have to take time to explain what important things you need her to do.

This is the way things are for any business. You're investing more than just time and money into this venture. When you get frustrated at people and wonder why they didn't do something you expected, remember where their loyalties lie. They may care, but they have to take care of themselves the same way you have to take care of yourself. It's not a "bad" thing, but it is one that we must remind ourselves periodically so that we don't take things so personally.

Don't Tear Down Another Provider to Build Yourself Up!

I need to stress this point.

--->It is not necessary to search for flaws or weaknesses in another provider in order to promote your business.

I have always been a "bright side of things" person, so this wasn't a challenge for me. I do notice that in efforts to sell themselves to parents, some women take a position of mud-slinging. You do not have to confirm nor deny any rumors that may have spread. This makes you look weak, petty, and malicious. If you can find fault with your colleagues and talk about things no one needs to know, how can a family trust you with their confidential information?

Focus on your strengths, and let the parents decide who they prefer. If you're bilingual, promote that. If you have a special talent, promote that. Not being selected does not make another provider more capable or "better" than you. It means another provider is seen as the best person to fit that family's needs at that time. There are more than 23 million children under age six in the U.S. that need care. Chances are good that you can find one or two since you can't very well care for every child that crosses your path! Maybe the other provider offers longer hours. Maybe the parent wants a small daycare, and you have a large one or vice versa. Don't stress over things you can't control. Focus on keeping your goals and presenting yourself properly so the family that will match you will recognize it and enroll with you.

Another thing to remember is that providers often network. We are independent businesses interacting and contacting other businesses for support, encouragement, and business practices. I have referred out clients to other providers many times with no problems. If they need infant care but I have no openings, I will refer people to someone I know who may have care.

1) Why not? I can't help them, so I might as well point them to someone or an agency that can. Obviously, they're calling because they don't already have someone. Even if you refer someone they already called, you've offered your help. It's the courteous thing to do.

2) It builds a professional relationship with your colleagues when they realize that you mentioned them by name to a potential family. They may (*may*), in turn, refer families to you in the future.

3) Parents may be deciding which provider to use, but raining negativity about another provider to these strangers puts a bad taste in their mouths to cross you off the list of potential caregivers.

4) Parents sometimes keep a list to remember which caregivers they prefer. You may be needed in the future for drop-in care. They may also ask to be on a waiting list or check back periodically to see if space is available.

5) Destroying the character of your colleague or trying to discount her business only hurts you. If I knock out your support system, it's going to hurt you when you fall.

Ask yourself this, "As a potential client, what can I offer me that would make me want to enroll? What would I want to see from me?" You could practice mock interviews with families. Create some practice profiles of families (ex. 2-year-old child, wears pull-ups, shy, never been in daycare, hours needed M, R, F – 9:30 – 4:30; T, W – 8:00 – 1:00, starting the day after tomorrow), and think about how you would handle that phone call. Would you accept half-day clients? What rate would you set? How could you help this child adjust to daycare?

Passage to ponder – Ecclesiates 4:9-10 KJV

This business can be isolating enough as it is. Provider support is good for everyone. It helps reduce stress, assists with trainings, helps get legislation passed, and can help to form strong friendships.

Your Personal Business Is Just That – Personal!

I understand you don't get to talk to adults often, and you love people, which is why you're in a caring profession. *BUT*…parents are not interested in knowing your life story and having you unload all of your problems on them. They came to you because they needed a service – not because they were lonely. You may like your clients and may eventually develop a friendship, but save your emotional drama for your support group or family and friends that know your situation. The more sensitive information you divulge to your clients, the harder it will be to enforce a policy when needed. Additionally, when it is time for that parent to leave your care, you may take it more personally because you tried to make the relationship different from what it was.

Imagine if you decide to confide in a client that you think your husband is cheating and that you and he got into a shouting match over the weekend. Why did you need to tell her that? It's not lying to not push your issues on her just because she came through the door. It's just keeping private issues private. She already has things going on in her life, so playing counselor to you is likely not what she had in mind for evening pickup. What happens if you're wrong and patch things up? You've just told this woman that you lost your cool, and maybe she thinks there's too much instability in your life to potentially expose her child to your problems. If another parent asks why she's leaving, is she going to feel like she has to maintain confidentiality? If a new parent asks if the mother would recommend you, what are the chances she'd say something like, "Oh, Carol's a great provider, but she and her husband are having a bunch of problems, so I don't know what's going to happen there. She already accused him of cheating." Now you've started your own rumor.

While you are handling business, keep a business attitude. Yes, be friendly. Sure, have light conversation and tell what is relevant to the parent. However, unless you already have an established friendship (ex. you talk on the phone or get together for lunch), don't add to the parents' problems with your own because you're not really looking for them to solve the problems. You just want someone to listen. Take your problems to someone who will listen, and keep things you don't want in the street in your house.

Passage to ponder – 1 Peter 5:6-7 KJV

Take your cares to the One Who always cares. It's not that your friends or clients don't care. Everyone has her own problems, and not everyone has a solution. God listens, and He always has a solution.

Section 4: Working with Families

Why Should I Provide Receipts?

Many providers don't think about providing receipts because they don't see it as important or because they don't plan on claiming it on taxes. If you're going to be caring for kids more than a day, it would benefit you to give receipts of some sort.

1) This tells parents that you are serious about your *business*. How many businesses do you know sell you a product or service without providing a receipt to prove you paid for it?

2) This helps you keep track of your profits and losses. If you have to refund payment for a couple of days, you can show it in your receipts.

3) When you need to report income for taxes, you can prove your income. If you need to get a loan, you need to be able

to prove you have a steady source of income, especially if you're trying to buy a house.

4) **Not providing receipts to parents doesn't keep them from reporting what they paid for daycare!**

Let me expand on #4. If you decide to charge 20% - 25% less a week hoping that they won't claim daycare on taxes and force you to pay taxes, you're setting yourself up to be screwed big time! Not only can that parent save more than several hundred dollars a year behind your deal, she can also turn around and claim her daycare payments under dependent care credit. If she fills out the information and writes "refused" for the tax ID portion, guess who's going to be questioned about unreported income? *You*!! To make matters worse, because you chose not to keep a record of how much you got paid, she can make up any amount she wants to claim, and the burden of proof is on you to show that you didn't get paid that much while also having to figure out your self-employment tax. Fun, fun, fun, right? There's nothing like a day at the auditor's office to spice up a week.

1) Now...let's add another problem to the pot for you. Suppose you decide to give multiple families this same discount. For simplicity's sake, let's say you state you would normally charge $100, but you decide to charge $75 to "give the mother a break." You watch 6 kids at a $25/week discount. $25 x 6 = $150/week in discounts. At 52 weeks per year, you have given away $7800 a year. You

believe it's okay because you earned $23,400 in income. If one or more people decide to claim dependent care credit, you're up for investigation, taxes, and any penalties.

a) Not only do you have to pay back taxes, you may have to pay a tax lawyer and accountant to assist you with the mess you created.

b) You have to take time off to get these things done, so you lose income for being closed. This puts your family in a tight spot because you don't know what to expect and have nothing set aside for it since you already spent your tax return.

c) The state is notified that you have been caring for several children in your home without proper certification. A DFCS (Department of Family & Child Services) inspector comes to your homes and discovers that you are out of compliance with state law and orders that you shut down operations, which means that you must tell all your families that they must find alternate care immediately.

d) $31,200 would have been your total earnings before taxes. Even if you were charged a high rate of 20% for self-employment taxes, without including deductions, you would come out with a higher income without trying to "get over."

2) Now, let me throw in another problem. Let's say you've done this periodically over the past couple years, and one

of your former clients just learned about dependent care tax credit and decides to file back taxes for the year prior. You've already got a flag raised for the current year, and now you have to try to remember what you did the year prior also.

Including back taxes, late fees, and penalties of daily and monthly compounded interest that you must repay for overpayments given to you, can you see how it just isn't worth the hassle to not report income? That's not considering any problems you have with the state behind operating your daycare out of compliance. You may see a short-term benefit, but you need to keep records so that you can settle everything ahead of time. Planning is the name of the game. Your job is to foresee obstacles that are around the corner.

Passage to ponder – Matt 6:19-21 KJV

Yes, money has its place, and we can use it wisely. Just don't lose sight of what's eternally important while handling financial matters.

Why Aren't These Parents Sending Supplies?

You may not agree with the style your clients use to care for their children, but I've found that most parents using home daycare truly care about their children. Give them the benefit of the doubt. They may have just forgotten. It's easy to get sidetracked rushing everyone in and out of the house, trying to remember everything the baby and school-agers need, prepare yourself for work, face morning and evening traffic, figure out how to get homework, dinner, and sleep in only to repeat the cycle the next day. Some parents just need to be reminded more often. For the most part, I don't believe parents are trying to scam you out of toothpaste or sippy cups that you keep in your home. It's just not high on their list of priorities. If it bothers you, or you feel like it's one more thing on a long list of things, feel free to find a tactful way to bring it up. Maybe all you need to do is write it down so they can see the reminder so they don't forget as soon as they leave the neighborhood.

Personally, this is not something I stress. Yes, I'd like people to remember supplies, but I know there have been days I forgot to replace wipes or bring milk for Cheerios. I am continually losing socks! So, yeah, I give people a break when they forget something I can provide. The main reason I don't harp on the little extras is because I don't know what goes on behind closed doors. Needy families may not come across as in need of something. It's also not something I ask. I offer assistance because I've had assistance offered to me. I know I would appreciate someone making the gesture. When I do, it's not necessarily because I believe they can't afford it, but it's available if they want it.

I remember a time when I was in need, but I don't remember saying anything and didn't ask anyone. I had lost everything and was forced to shop at 50% specials at thrift shops. My children were growing, and the little bit we had we couldn't use, especially since the seasons had changed. I remember deciding to give the clothes we couldn't use and just trusting God that I'd be able to buy more clothes soon. The next day, I was given several pairs of shoes and a couple dozen dresses, outfits, and coats (I still have some). When I picked up my children from daycare, the provider asked if I wanted some clothes another parent had given away. There were 6 giant bags of clothes that I used for everyone! I can't tell you what it meant to me to have someone hold clothes and say, "Wait! I know someone who might be able to use these." I think I cried with excitement the whole week. Thinking about it these many years later still warms my heart.

That's why I don't consider it a big deal to provide extra blankets or wipes, if needed. It's not like I'm buying cases of formula. I can get small blankets on sale, and they stay with me. Non-scented wipes aren't that expensive to keep on hand.

If you're providing food and get the feeling that a child doesn't get to eat much at home due to financial circumstances, then I would suggest making sure you plan menus with him in mind. Maybe you'd like heavier meal selections for Mondays when he returns and Fridays before he goes home. *If* you're going to approach a family, please be courteous as this is a very sensitive topic. You might want to have a flyer that you pass out to every family (so no one feels singled out) letting them know about the resources available in the community. Offer availability to help your families locate assistance, if needed. Remember that you are partners with the parents to look out for the child's well-being. If the child is hungry or the family can't get their basic needs met, it will affect everyone – even you. If you were the one in that situation, would you want someone to make help available to you, or would you rather struggle and hope you don't drown as your troubles build up?

Passage to ponder – Matt 25:31-46

If you can be a blessing to someone, do so.

Extend Grace...At Least Once

We have a tendency to get into our own routines and expect everyone else to kind of fall in line or move out of the way. I notice people tend to be focused on themselves because they know what is going on with their situations at all times. Makes sense, right? You know what you need to do each day for care, and you believe you've expressed that clearly to parents. Here's the thing. Life happens.

Most parents mean well, so I encourage providers to try to work with parents even on something major at least once. If it becomes a pattern, then you'll need to set that straight. For most families, I don't believe it will be a problem and will help strengthen the relationship later.

I can think of a couple instances where I regret not giving someone the benefit of the doubt. In one instance, I hadn't heard from one family for 10 straight days (Friday until the Monday of the second week). I have a policy that includes a time-frame for days without contacting me and non-payment. I removed the family from my enrollment due to non-contact, non-payment, and to make room for a family that had stated they wanted to enroll their infant when

I had space. The family I had let go was a family with four children, and I cared for the three youngest.

I was a state-registered provider and accepted children through social services (only available to state-certified providers), and this family was one of my clients. When I was contacted by the case worker about attendance, I informed her that the mother told me she hadn't called due to her child being ill. Being a fairly new provider in that area and not understanding why someone wouldn't call me all that time, I didn't think I should bend on this rule. While we had had some small bumps previously, it just never occurred to me that the mother may have:

1) been telling the truth and forgot she needed to call to keep me updated or

2) been too embarrassed to discuss the truth of her situation with me and said what she thought would be acceptable.

In hindsight, I know that the family had had many difficulties with living situations, sickness, and employment. I probably made things much more difficult for her not just letting her back that week. It is extremely hard to find care for two part-time preschoolers and an infant, get an older child to school who also needs after-school care, work a minimum wage job, and work hours that allow you to drop off and pick up everyone before late fees kick in. Honestly, I've been thinking about that situation all morning and have been sick about it. So, I hope that my mistake in judgment will help someone else consider that parents make mistakes, too. While you may be thinking about money you *could* get with another client, you need to remember that that's not money you actually have yet. Daycare is built on relationships. If the children fit well in your program, and lapses in judgment is not a normal occurrence, you would do better in the long run to let it go. Even if you have to make payment arrangements for the missed week or count it as a business loss, it's better than "x" number of weeks without pay from the family you believe you could enroll but don't (and then have to start building a brand, new relationship with someone else).

Passage to ponder - Matt 18:21-35

God has extended you much grace, should you not extend a portion to someone you see could use it?

What If I Make a Mistake?

Oh! Don't worry about that! You'll screw up *plenty* of times. You'll make bad decisions, will have lapses in judgment, will cave in on your policies at least once, will regret opening your mouth, and will wonder if you should even be doing this. Once you do that, you'll have learned a huge lesson, will be wiser for it, and will become a little stronger because of it. Hopefully, you'll have support and will be able to laugh it off later.

Your first week and each new enrollment are going to be challenges. The 20 minutes you had scheduled for circle time may finish in 5 minutes. Lunch takes longer than planned because you forgot to preheat the oven. Dinner gets changed because you didn't thaw the meat. You'll pour juice into the wrong cup and have to wash it out and find another drink. You'll schedule 15 minutes to get from the front door to the van for a field trip but forget to add another 15 minutes for putting on shoes and another 5 minutes for the one who suddenly remembers he needs to go potty. Any number of things can happen, and you'll continue to make mistakes through the rest of your career. However, you'll make fewer mistakes as you learn and will likely make them fewer times. Don't let your "what ifs" stop your ambitions.

Miko Marsh

Passage to ponder Phil 3:13-14

Just keep pressing forward! Sprinting or crawling forward is still progress.

Section 5: Final Thoughts

- Open the blinds and let in the sun. Sunshine is great! It's free light, it brightens a room, and it's a source of vitamin D. You're going to be inside the house most of the time. Opening the blinds and windows will help fight off depression that can occur.

- Go on field trips. It's a great way to expose the children to something different, help guide them in appropriate outside behavior, and a great reason to get out of the house.

- Do something different with your hair and make yourself pretty. I know it can be difficult to want to dress up when you don't feel like you get to go anywhere, but the boost it gives you is phenomenal.

- Plan things just for your family. Earning a living is nice, but don't neglect your family in the process – especially if you became a provider to be there for them!

- If a baby does a major first at your daycare (ex. first steps), don't steal the joy from the parents rushing to tell what happened. Many parents, especially first-time and single mothers, feel guilty about having to work away from their child. They trust you and appreciate what you do, but getting to see major firsts is something they want to experience. Plus, the baby may have done it at home. Try to hold off your excitement, and wait for the mother to tell you what she got to see. Then, share in her happiness (Notice I said share in the happiness of the mother getting to see this first because it's a first to her and very special. Don't steal her joy by trumping it.) It may be easier said than done because we love to give parents great reports, but try (really, *REALLY* hard).

- Do what you can to help parents feel more connected through your care. Invite them for parent days, help children make gifts for them, or encourage them to go home and do something special for the family. Parents sometimes feel guilty or jealous about needing someone else to watch their child. They are stressed and often frustrated with life's problems. Sometimes an emailed picture, an "I love you" gift from the child, or a periodic parent's night out would be very helpful. Try to imagine yourself in your clients' shoes occasionally, and think of what you would want someone to do for you based on your circumstances…then do something.

- Change the knobs on your bathroom doors to those without a lock or those that have a single, grooved line across the middle. Tape a nickel to the wall above the doorpost so that you can access it, and use it to unlock the door in case a child accidentally locks himself inside. This will help you get to the child faster.

- Turn the hot water off in the bathroom accessible to children so they don't burn themselves washing their hands.

- Make sure you have a support system in place for the hard times (and for the funny ones, too).

- Find a mentor. The preference would be someone nearby that could easily assist, but some get a little nervous about other providers asking them questions due to some people trying to take ideas and clients. You may need to call someone outside your area for questions.

- Enjoy the ride! The ups, the downs, the frustrations, the surprises, the hugs, the giggles, the growth, the lessons learned, and the "thank yous" are all worth the venture into your new field.

And...in case no one has said it yet,

"Welcome to the wonderful world of daycare!"

About the Author

Miko Marsh is an author, speaker, and instructor. She has a degree in psychology with a minor in counseling from Old Dominion University and college certification in Early Childhood Care Education from Chattahoochee Technical College. She worked directly with individuals in behavioral health facilities to assist and support individuals with various disabilities and/or disorders and operated her own business as a private childcare provider.

She primarily writes nonfiction and children's books. Her author credits include books related to business, faith, personal transformation, and children. She enjoys supporting others, helping them to find areas in which they can shine, and seeing people of all ages and abilities reach their individual goals.

Other Books by This Author

I truly appreciate you reading my book! If you found something of value here, please take a moment to leave a review for the next person. You can also find me on other platforms.

Website: http://www.writeheartpublishing.com
Facebook: http://www.facebook.com/WriteHeartPublishing
Instagram: http://www.instagram.com/writeheartpublishing

Please visit your favorite online retailer to discover other books by Miko Marsh:

Self-help/Personal Transformation:
- Living with Jezebel: An In-Depth Look at the Queen of Narcissism, Her Tactics, and Three Generations of Destruction (also available in Spanish)
- You Don't Want Success: Demolishing Excuses Used to Prevent You from Achieving Your Goals
- Stop Surviving and LIVE! How I Changed My Poverty Mindset to Control My Future

<u>Caregiving</u>:

- Introduction to Childcare: An Overview for the Aspiring Professional Caregiver

- Daycare Days for Parents: Answers & Tips from a Provider

<u>Children's books</u>:

- Charles Meets a Fire Marshal

- Grandma B. & Me (Books 1-4)

www.ingramcontent.com/pod-product-compliance
Lightning Source LLC
Chambersburg PA
CBHW080248200526
45166CB00021B/1312